CONSIGNMENT BOUTIQUE PRIMER

(Entrepreneurship for the Lady Who Loves Apparel and People)

By

Nimi Wanek

and

Ken Meyer

MEYER-MAN BOOKS

Library of Congress Card Number 92-90837
ISBN 0-9632984-0-2

Printed in the U. S. A.

THIS BOOK IS
DEDICATED
TO

ANDY WANEK
AND
BARBARA MEYER

MEYER-MAN BOOKS

TABLE OF CONTENTS

LIST OF EXHIBITS

EXHIBIT 1. TJ's Unique Boutique

INTRODUCTION

Hundreds, if not thousands, of books have been written about business management; many devoted to specific topics--marketing, finance, retail, advertising, insurance, etc.

Very few have investigated the start-up and operation of a consignment clothing store; much less a consignment boutique!

CONSIGN: to send goods to an agent for sale or custody. A **BOUTIQUE** is a fashionable specialty shop for women; a small retail store. A **PRIMER** IS A "BEGINNING BOOK." The **CONSIGNMENT BOU-TIQUE PRIMER** breaks new ground.

The dearth of books on the subject is not surprising since the privately-owned, consignment clothing store phenomenon is barely twenty years old.

The bibliography at the back of this book reveals the story. Thanks to the Division of Library and Information Services, Florida Department of State, for their assistance in research.

Please meet **NIMI WANEK**....

Most of the information contained within the covers of this book comes from Nimi Wanek. Her first-hand experience is credible.

She relates, "My neighbor, TJ Shouton, a lovely lady from the Netherlands, owned and operated **TJ's Unique Boutique** in Madeira Beach, Florida.

"One day my son, Shane, buddy of TJ's son, remarked, 'Mom, as much as you like clothes, why don't you work in her store?' The idea was born. I asked her and she said, 'Yes!'

"It was that simple. About a year later, TJ offered to sell the store to me. This was a much larger decision!

"My husband, Andy, who only recently had started his pawnshop, was very supportive. So, off to the bank we went. Fortunately, we were able to arrange a loan and swing the deal.

"Additional moral support came from Jean Smith, Andy's mother, who had years of successful retail experience. Her help was of tremendous value.

"Buying a going business puts on a lot of pressure. You know it is profitable so you want to keep it growing. After doing some homework, I checked out a few items with our attorney. Actually, I just followed my instincts. I owned TJ's UNIQUE BOUTIQUE!

"Fortunately, I am somewhat artistic and do have a flair for coordinating clothes. TJ taught me to make the store inviting. It must be neat and tidy. Lay it out so it is pleasing to the eye but, above all , keep it clean!

"People work very hard for their money and most of them value a bargain. There are a lot of wise shoppers out there."

Four years later, Nimi encountered a lease problem which prompted her to move the store. She selected space in nearby Seminole, Florida--off the beaches. In 1987 she sold the store to Shelley Antonucci; who, in 1990, sold it to its present owner, Nancy Robinson.

Our thanks to Nancy, who supplied many of the exhibits and granted permission for the photography...plus other helpful tips.

Please meet **KEN MEYER**...

After spending 22 years in sales and sales management with one of the nation's largest life insurance companies, he was benched due to legal-blindness. Thanks to modern technology, he is back to writing books. This is his sixth.

Ken's practical experience in direct sales and general business management blends well with Nimi's hands-on experience.

Please meet the **CONSIGNMENT CONTRACT**...

The heart of a consignment store is the <u>consignment contract.</u> Terms are spelled out in the contract which entrust goods to a dealer for sale with the consignor retaining ownership of them until sold. The dealer pays only when and if the goods are sold. See sample in Exhibit 2.

Use it well. Enjoy the profitable and rewarding career of entrepreneur!

<u>EXHIBIT 2.</u> The Contract

T.J.'s UNIQUE BOUTIQUE

Fashions On Consignment

9148 Seminole Boulevard
Seminole, FL 34642
Phone (813) 397-1073

CONTRACT FOR CONSIGNMENT

CONTRACT BETWEEN: T.J.'s UNIQUE BOUTIQUE and;   CLIENT CODE #: _____

CLIENT NAME: _____   PHONE: ( ) _____

STREET ADDRESS: _____

CITY: _____ STATE: _____ ZIP: _____

TERMS:

» Client will receive 50% of ACTUAL SELLING PRICE of items.

» T.J.'s UNIQUE BOUTIQUE reserves the right to discount merchandise to sell slower moving items or to promote special sales.

» T.J.'s UNIQUE BOUTIQUE is NOT RESPONSIBLE for reminding client of the contract expiration date.

» Contract is for three months. Upon contract expiration, unsold articles not picked up by client become property of T.J.'s Unique Boutique. Any money due client must be picked up within one month of the contract expiration date or it is forfeited.

» T.J.'s UNIQUE BOUTIQUE is NOT RESPONSIBLE for damage or loss due to handling, fire, water damage, pilfering, or burglary.

Read and understood by: _____
                                   Client Signature   *Date Signed*

Articles received by: _____

Thank you for your business!!
T.J.'s UNIQUE BOUTIQUE

EXHIBIT 3. Part of a Strip Center

1

CARDINAL RULES

"The business of America is business."
-Calvin Coolidge

Look before you leap! Failure to follow these commandments when starting your consignment boutique carries a severe penalty. On the other hand, careful planning assures bountiful reward. The CARDINAL RULES will be explained in succeeding chapters.

The CARDINAL RULES are not listed in order of importance--the correct response to all of them is absolutely vital to your success!

CARDINAL RULE NO. 1

<u>Does retailing fit you?</u> Notice, we did not ask, "Do you fit in?" It is unfair to expect either you or retailing to change once you open your doors, thus it is vital to determine if you will like this kind of work!

Everyone likes working with people to some extent, but do you like to PLEASE people? Have you ever worked in retail before? Do you enjoy working with clothing? In other words, does your personal dress reflect your being clothes conscious?

Pleasing customers must give you a lot of job satisfaction; more than merely a means to make a buck.

CARDINAL RULE NO. 2

<u>Location.</u> A tested axiom says, The three most important things in starting a store are: location, location and location!" Unlike a service business. which can take its service to the customer, your boutique must be convenient to the costumer.

Location must be elevated to No. 1 consideration. A poor location will kill the business faster than any other enemy of profit.

CARDINAL RULE NO. 3

<u>Capitalization.</u> Most small businesses fail for either of two reasons; poor management or under-capitalization. The latter means not having enough money to weather the storm until you can start making money.

In Chapter 10 you will calculate required start-up capital. R. Manning Brown, late Chairman of the Board of the giant New York Life Insurance Company, said, "We have money for <u>anything,</u> but we do not have money for <u>everything!"</u> Adequate capital buys time to sharpen skills.

CARDINAL RULE NO. 4

<u>Product Specialization.</u> You cannot be every-thing to everyone in a small store. Word-of-mouth travels faster when satisfied customers can brag about your specialty!

A boutique specializes in stylish women's cloth-ing. Some stores have even specialized in large sizes.

Build an <u>identity.</u>

While becoming known for a specialty, you will grow in your skill of selecting the right garments within that special market.

CARDINAL RULE NO. 5

<u>Your</u> <u>Competition.</u> Survey the community; carefully study the competition. What kind of shops exist? What are their specialties? If you plan to stick to good "labels," what are the others doing? Where are the Goodwill and Salvation Army stores located?

Study their prices. It will help you understand your own pricing. Remember, Goodwill-type stores sell donated, not consigned, goods. You can price above them and still attract the market-segment which wants higher quality merchandise.

CARDINAL RULE NO. 6

<u>Low</u> <u>Overhead.</u> Use every opportunity to keep overhead low; upgrade later when profitable. For example, start with a used cash register. Keep the phone system simple. Shut off lights in unoccupied

dressing rooms and rest rooms.

Can your spouse, or other family members, work part-time? When needing to hire help, look for older, part-time people; a strong work ethic and reduced absenteeism is the reward.

CARDINAL RULE NO. 7

Expect to Work Long Hours. Post regular store hours and never vary! But, expect to work much longer. You will be your own boss, but no 40-hour work week!

When you hire part-time help, put them on a regular schedule whenever possible. Remember, your own performance level must be monitored carefully; take some time off now and then.

CARDINAL RULE NO. 8

Perfect a Complete Business Management System. Establish proper inventory controls. What is selling best? How often are consignors paid? Who handles the bookkeeping system? Who maintains it? Who computes taxes?

First time business owners often fail to realize the need for business management; beware the trap!

Install a system that tells you which garments are moving and which ones are not. When should seasonal items be displayed? How often should the window be trimmed?

CARDINAL RULE NO. 9

<u>Source of Supply.</u> First, set a standard and have the courage to stick to it. Seek consignors from the affluent sector. Moderately priced, high quality apparel is a sure-fire winner.

Accept only clean clothing; inspect each garment carefully for stains, tears, or missing buttons. Suggestion: inspect clothing in the presence of the consignor.

Keep the inventory fresh. Place a time limit on each item. Have a game plan; if it doesn't sell, move it out!

CARDINAL RULE NO. 10

<u>Develop a Personality for your Store.</u> Start by

picking a name that reflects what you intend to do. If you are going to take faded, stained sweat suits, don't call it a boutique!

Your attitude toward customers will be reflected by employees. Let your smile become a fixture and, remember, when an error does occur, the two magic words in the English language are, "I'm sorry."

The customer that stays is the customer that pays. Patronage goes where it is welcome and comes back to where it is appreciated.

2

LOCATION

"No man can see all with his own eyes or
do all with his own hands."
-Samuel Johnson: The Idler, No. 19.

The CARDINAL RULE of "Location, location and location," is sacro sanct. Here are key factors to consider when selecting space.

1. **Foot traffic.** Where are women shopping? Point: a boutique is slanted to the working woman's market. Where is the foot-traffic?

Is there a strip shopping center that has a bank, a cleaners, a gift shop , or other stores which attract the same customers you want? Avoid new centers because rent will be high and foot traffic has yet to be established.

When a good spot is found, spend time on the parking lot--observe the foot traffic!

2. Established shopping center. There are other advantages to the older shopping center. Rent will be lower. Talk to present tenants; is the landlord fulfilling his end of the lease?

3. Amount of space. A common strip center allocation is 20' x 60', or 1,200 square feet. For starters, this is adequate. Avoid as much remodeling cost as possible. Hang tough in negotiations; persuade the landlord to pick up as many costs as possible!

4. Calculating rent. Rent is usually quoted by dollars per square foot on an annual basis. For example, $8.00 per foot means $8.00 x 1,200 square feet, or $9,600 annual rental. $800 per month.

5. **Term of Lease.** Try for one year and don't settle for more than two. There are as many leases as there are landlords. When he says it is a "standard" lease, let an attorney confirm it!

For example, Nimi moved TJ's Unique Boutique upon expiration of a lease term due to a fight with the landlord over a roof problem later won in court. The lease said he was to take care of outside repairs, but he billed each tenant for the cost of roofing repairs.

6. **Renewal Option.** When you pick right, you want to stay. Study your rights carefully. If there is an escalator clause which governs rent increases, is it reasonable?

7. **When to Open.** Don't start your occupancy until ready to open the doors. Rent is fixed overhead and must be paid regardless of income from sales. Paying rent on vacant space is a sure loss. Hold space preparation time to a bare minimum.

8. **Utilities.** Insist upon having your own electric meter. If forced to share common heating and air conditioning

systems, assure basic protection is spelled out in the lease.

9. <u>**Maintenance.**</u> What is the landlord obligated to provide? Ask neighboring tenants to share their past experience. Being forewarned is being forearmed.

10. <u>**Sign.**</u> Whose responsibility? What does the lease say? Avoid exotic or hard-to-read lettering.

11. <u>**Parking.**</u> Availability? Liability? Maintenance? Adequacy?

12. **The** <u>**DON'T LIST.**</u> Has the landlord loaded the lease with "Don't do this, don't do that" items?

EXHIBIT 4. Sales Counter

3

PREPARING THE STORE

"Expenses properly managed make half an income."
-Iben Tibbon, Izavah

Assume the site is found for your boutique. It is 20' wide and 60' deep with a display window facing East. Previously occupied, there is a partition at the rear of the shop. The 10' x 20' room includes a rest room. The remaining space served as storage for the previous tenant.

One thousand square feet remains for display layout. Ceiling is in and contains recessed lighting. The walls are painted; not the best shape but acceptable. The tile floor is neutral color and in good condition. The landlord steadfastly refuses to carpet.

This particular strip center uses a uniform, lighted style sign. Cost to redo with new store name is approximately $500. Street numbers are already on the door--no charge.

CAUTION: What kind of store are you going to begin with? Are you going to rough it, go first class, or settle for somewhere in-between? Commit before costing it out. Unless you have unlimited capital, prepare for compromise.

The boutique's appearance is important; however, imagination, ingenuity and hard work can create a pleasant shopper's environment at minimal cost.

Learn to use the "what if" technique! For instance, what if a real bargain can be found on racks? The savings could permit new paint and other wall decoration. There are numerous decisions to be made; some trade-offs. Use this chapter to form a check-list.

Here are some suggestions which, when totaled, can provide a ball-park cost figure.

FIXTURES

SALES COUNTER

Shop used furniture stores and find a piece you like; convert it into a sales counter. Please note Exhibit 4. The glass showcase and sales counter are arranged in "L" shape to discourage customers from moving behind the counter. The sales counter is a formica top added to an old knee-hole desk.

The sales counter also contains the cash drawer.

DRESSING ROOMS

"Partition and panel;" construct your own unless you can afford a contractor. 3' x 4' should be adequate. Unless ceiling light panels are directly above dressing rooms, use portable lighting.

Place hooks on walls. Install full-length mirror on back wall. Add a shelf for purse, packages, etc. Curtains can be home made. Rods are simple, expandable rods purchased at dime store.

Hair nets and tissue are provided for the personal protection of the customer...a courtesy.

Exhibit 5 portrays a cheval glass standing outside dressing rooms. It adds a touch of class as well as additional full-length mirror. If space and money permit, a three-way mirror is a great idea.

CLOTHING RACKS

Check Yellow Page listings under "Display Fixtures and Materials," "Liquidators," and "Furniture, Used" for companies dealing in store fixtures and equipment.

Note the circular racks in Exhibit 6. They are convenient and more customers can be accomodated. An old-fashioned halltree can serve as a handbag or hat rack.

Plan on $400-500 for purchase of used racks.

SHELVING

The shoe rack, shown in Exhibit 7, was constructed with good lumber purchased from a local building supply store. Shelving above the racks, lining each wall, is displayed in Exhibit 8. (Note the small stereo system atop the shelving. A simple music system for customer "easy" listening.)

Lattice-type display, shown in Exhibit 9, is home-made. Purchase it locally, paint or stain for accent and attach to wall.

HANGERS

Before you buy, make a decision on the kind of hanger to be used. Stay uniform. Don't mix wire with plastic, etc.

Again, check the used stores. If not available, ask for direction to specialty house dealing in retail store supplies. It may be a good investment to go to new hangers.

OFFICE SUPPLIES

TO BE PURCHASED

Sales book, pens, pencils, paper clips, stapler, index cards. bookkeeping journal; all can be purchased at local office supply store.

TO BE PRINTED

Consignment Contract. (See Exhibit 2 and Chapter 4.)

Business Cards. Color catches the eye. Order 1,000. Use liberally.

EXHIBIT 5. Cheval Glass

EXHIBIT 6. Circular Racks

Article Acceptance Form. (See Exhibit 10 and Chapter 5.) Make this a separate form or part of consignment contract?

Grand Opening Flyer. Plus other sales promotion hand-outs. (see Chapter 8.)

Tags. In six colors; year supply (2,000) of each. (See Chapter 5.)

Suggestion: Develop rapport with proprietor of a quickie print shop. There may be a time when you need a favor.

OTHER ITEMS

Rubber Stamp. 4 lines. Self-inking type preferred.

File Cabinet. Cardboard file box will suffice in beginning. Watch classified ads.

Handling Money. Cash drawer or cash register? Nimi found an old-fashioned cash register through a friend; it became a conversation piece.

Calculator. Is there a spare around the house?

Tagging Supplies. Tagging gun and barbs or tagging needle; buy from supply house that had the hangers.

Merchandise Bags. Paper or plastic? Order three sizes to avoid waste.

Gift Boxes. In assorted size; a courtesy that keeps them coming back.

Mailing Supplies. When catering to tourist trade, Nimi found it beneficial to mail purchases "back home" for client!

Display Supplies. New mannequins are quite expensive; look for second-hand. Purchase miniature T-stands for blouse and top display.

Reminder; Once committed to starting a consignment boutique, start watching the newspaper ads for liquidation sales and/or auctions. Good fortune tends to smile on those who are vigilant and alert.

CREDIT CARD

Contact the bank where you plan to have your business account and make arrangements for VISA and MASTERCARD.

Securing the machines for handling credit card purchases and a supply of tickets will cost around $100. Plan for this in your "Start-Up Cost." (See Chapter 10).

EXHIBIT 7. Shoe Rack

EXHIBIT 8. A Modest Sereo System

4

INVENTORY

"Thy clothes are all the soul thou hast."
-Beaumont and Fletcher: Honest Man's
Fortune V.iii.

Inventory is the name given to an asset of a business. There are two general types--direct and indirect. **Direct inventory** in a retail business is composed of goods purchased for resale. Consigned goods are not carried on the books as an asset, but are treated separately. **Indirect inventory** includes all supplies needed to carry on the business and are not purchased for resale.

PURCHASED GOODS

There may be times when garments, jewelry or accessories are purchased for resale rather than taken on consignment. One example, **advertise.** When starting from scratch, a simple method of acquiring an initial inventory is to advertise for used clothing. Buy it outright and store it in your garage until ready to open the boutique.

Garage sales offer another purchase source. Keep tuned to the affluent communities and hit the sales early! After you are open for business it will become more difficult to attend such sales but, perhaps, a relative can be trained to do it.

Close-outs at retail boutiques are another fount. When stock is reduced to one or two of a kind in a size, they often want to unload them for a fraction of cost. Display of a few NEW items, tags still attached, improves rack appearance. SUGGESTION: Develop store managers to call you first when they have garments for disposal. Build a steady flow of quality merchandise.

Estate sales are also an excellent inventory

possibility. Not only are the garments usually top quality, but you can often convince the heirs conducting the sale to unload a batch of goods for a reduced price.

Utilize all the above methods; it is not difficult to amass an inventory ready for the GRAND OPENING!

Note we did not include **FLEA MARKETS** in the above group of sources. They vary greatly by area. Might be a good source for accessories. Watch out for <u>dated</u> items: keep all goods as current as possible.

CONSIGNED GOODS

Once your store is in operation, the principal source of merchandise will be consignors. The **CONSIGNMENT CONTRACT** is the heart of this phase of your enterprise. Understand it completely and prepare yourself to explain it countless times...thoroughly.

The contract form used by TJ's Unique Boutique is about as simple as one can make it and still get the job done. Please note Exhibit 2.

Observe the company heading and the client information section. The **client code number** is assigned when the consignor initially brings items to your store. This is a continuing contract. The client code number is used to identify consigned articles, control payments, and other uses.

Terms of the contract are kept to a bare minimum and are exceedingly simple. First, **Payment Percentage.** TJ's gives the consignor 50%, period! Ideas abound. For instance, one store owner might want to offer a higher percentage based on volume of sales. Would this encourage the consignor to bring in more articles? Do you need more merchandise?

The second clause says TJ's will do all the pricing, period! If you desire to have the consignor participate in the pricing, draft the clause to include such arrangement.

The third clause: TJ's waiver of responsibility for reminding consignor of **contract expiration.** Without this clause, you are tackling a mountain of paper work and responsibility to notify all consignors at or before the date of expiration of their contracts.

Clause four spells out the time frame and what happens to goods or money upon contract expiration. TJ's uses months rather than days. It is much simpler and eliminates a lot of day-counting!

Again, this clause can be written to reflect how you want to run your business. Some owners prefer to work on a shorter cycle to create a faster turnover.

What if you want to subsequently change the arrangement? Have new contract forms prepared and from a certain date, have consignors sign a new contract bearing the new terms. Do not make it retroactive.

The last clause is another **disclaimer** which is understandable. Normally, consigned goods are not insured against the perils listed. It is a good idea to put the disclaimer in the contract.

It is recommended you consult your attorney before printing the contract. There may be state laws or local ordinances which must be given legal consideration.

File the store's copy of each contract alphabetically by last name.

EXHIBIT 9. A Sitting Room, No Less!

EXHIBIT 10. Articles Acceptance Tool

T.J.'s UNIQUE BOUTIQUE

NAME _Jane Doe_

CLIENT CODE # _D-2_

TAG COLOR _Blue_

EFFECTIVE DATE _4/2/92_

EXPIRATION DATE _7/2/92_

NO.	ARTICLES RECEIVED	SIZE	PRICE	SOLD	AMT.	DUE	PD.
1	Dress - lt. blue/white	8	15.00	4/4	15.00	7.50	4/8
2	Blouse - pink, ruffled (ls.)	10	8.00				
3	Slacks - tan (Liz)	10	12.00	4/6	12.00	6.00	4/8
4	Nitie - white, short	S	7.00				
5	Skirt - gray, pleated	10	8.00				
6	Earrings - rhinestone (clip)	—	4.00	4/4	4.00	2.00	4/8
7	Necklace - white beads	—	2.00				
8	Shoes - black pumps	7½	8.00	4/4	8.00	4.00	4/8
9	Dress - long, red silk	8	40.00				
10	Dress red/white stripe	8	12.00				

T.J.'s UNIQUE BOUTIQUE

NAME _____

CLIENT CODE # _____

TAG COLOR _____

EFFECTIVE DATE _____

EXPIRATION DATE _____

NO.	ARTICLES RECEIVED	SIZE	PRICE	SOLD	AMT.	DUE	PD.
1							
2							
3							
4							
5							
6							
7							

5

ACCESSORIES

"A woman craves for jewelry."

-Eleazar.T:Ketubot, 65a.

Nimi says, "Accessories can make or break you. When a customer has picked a garment, always draw attention to a handbag, jewelry item, or a matching pair of shoes.

"I displayed all accessories in the rear of the store near the sales counter. I found ladies who bring in clothing often do not want to buy clothing. But, they will see a pair of shoes or a purse they like. They are getting rid of clothing but may need accessories.

"I also displayed lingerie, pajamas, and such items where they could easily be seen. Many times when a customer cannot find a dress or a suit to their liking, they will pick up some lingerie. You must be able to satisfy their urge to buy."

BELTS

Salvage every presentable belt you come upon; whether it be leather, plastic, cord, or elastic. Don't worry about the colors when collecting. Become a belt specialist. Often the mere addition of a belt can change the entire look of the garment. Gradually train your customers to do likewise by doing it first!

GLOVES

Do not assume gloves are strictly for evening wear. Nimi says, "You might be amazed at the gloves I sold....despite our Florida climate. Call it the 'Michael Jackson syndrome' if you will. Stock them? It is a judgment call."

HANDBAGS

Be particular in accepting handbags and

purses. Make sure the lining is not ripped or soiled, fasteners are in proper working order, and straps are not cracked or peeling. In other words, would you buy it for your personal wardrobe?

Determine the kind of rack to be used for display. Space will govern, to some extent, the quantity to be kept on hand.

HATS

Will hats sell in your area? If you think so, try them. Idea: create a wall display rather than give up priority space.

HOSIERY

With today's fascination for colors, hosiery is no longer a taboo for your store. Nimi says, "Learn to color coordinate. Keep your soft tones with lighter colors and evening tones with dark colors."

JEWELRY

Nimi says, "My husband, Andy, is a pawnbroker

with marked expertise in jewelry. We thought it might be a good idea to stock some really good items, but backed out when we calculated the risk of burglary. As a result, I ended up concentrating on less-expensive, costume jewelry."

Have a display case, if at all possible, because ladies are accustomed to seeing jewelry in a display case. Visit a shopping mall and notice how costume jewelry is being displayed.

As with other accessories, develop the habit of asking each customer, "May I show you a necklace to go with the blue dress?"

Nimi says, "The proper piece of jewelry will turn an inexpensive garment into a class item."

LINGERIE

Nimi says, "Proper undergarments give the customer a pyschological lift. Don't hesitate to advise them.

"For example, a clinging sweater will lay smoother if a camisole or full slip is worn; making the person look slimmer and more attractive to the eye."

MUFFS

Nimi says, "We just don't see them in Florida, but I suspect they would be in demand up north." What do you think?

SCARVES

Scarves are often over-looked as an accent piece. As with belts, collect many because they vary so much in style, color, size and fabric. Look for hand-rolled edges to determine if it is of better quality. Again, habitually draw attention to them for many ladies are not accustomed to wearing them.

Nimi says, "The 90's have brought scarves from the bottom of the drawer to the top, They are being used as belts, sashes, hair berets, dickies or turtle necks, among other things."

SHAWLS

Keep a few in stock. Like hats, are they in vogue in your area?

SHOES

Keep the inventory under control. Best way is to allocate limited space. Accept only those which are clean and in good repair.

There is such a wide range of color and styles, it is easy to let the inventory get out of control.

TIP: Coordinate with your clothing. For example, if you carry few party dresses, don't load up on party shoes; on the contrary, if your main market is working women, carry more for them.

Try to carry a couple pair of each size, but more in the popular sizes (7 thru 9).

EXHIBIT 11. The Tag: Heart of the System
(Actual Size)

No. _____
STYLE _____
SIZE _____
PRICE _____
- - - - - - - - -
No. _____
STYLE _____
SIZE _____
PRICE _____

6

ACCEPTING ARTICLES

"One had as good be out of the
world as of the fashion."

-Colley Gibber:
Love's Last Shift.

Despite alternate sources of articles discussed in preceding chapters, the primary, and continuing, source of fashionable clothing for your boutique will be customers. They become the "Acres of Diamonds in your Own Backyard."

Nimi says, "Learn each customer by name. It is flattering to be called by name when appearing for the 10:30 appointment. Also, let them know you have set aside a special time just for them.

"Be extremely careful when rejecting clothing. Unfortunately, you must do it because some will be out-dated, stained, torn, frayed, missing buttons, have broken zippers and what not.

"Merely explain your store has set standards and, unfortunately, these garments just do not measure up. Do not lower your standards and accept apparel just because she is a sweet lady! She, no doubt, thinks they are nice, but don't cave in. Stick in there. Nothing will ruin your store faster than taking clothing that won't sell!

CODE NUMBER AND CODE BOOKS

Each consignor is assigned a code number. Her name and number is listed in a code book. Nimi used a three-ring binder for each letter of the alphabet; eventually, 26 code books.

Please note Exhibit 10; Jane Doe has a code number, D-2. "D," first letter of the last name, leads you to the right book. "2" happens to be the second person in the book.

To assign a code, pull the binder with the consignor's last initial, select the next number to be assigned. Never duplicate a code number!

<u>NOTE:</u> Nimi combined the CONSIGNMENT CON-
TRACT and ARTICLES RECEIPT on a single, full-page
form, 3-hole punched. Exhibits 2 and 10 show current
forms.

The reason for having a one-page form is to
assure there is a current contract always on file.
Names, addresses, etc. change; the code number
never changes.

All article receipts are thus filed in the code
book, so everything is in one place; simplicity plus.

STEP-BY-STEP

Let us follow Nimi, step-by-step, as she accepts
articles from a consignor.

1. <u>Appointment.</u> Morning hours preferable.
Allow minimum of 30 minutes. Ask at first contact,
"How many articles will you have?" Allow more time
where necessary. Allowing ample time will avoid frus-
trating over-lap of appointments. Be flexible enough to

accommodate working women, emergencies, etc.

Nimi says, "I suggest the consignor look around the store while I complete the check-in. If a first-time customer, consult proper code book and assign a code number. If a regular consignor, ask her for her code number. If she doesn't remember it, look it up.."

2. **Inspect** and **Price.** Inspect each garment, then enter specifics in space provided on the Articles Acceptance form. See Exhibit 10. Assign the price you determine-- based upon style, condition, dating and over-all appearance.

3. **Service Fee.** The use of service fees (designed to offset cost of paperwork) is debatable. Think it through carefully before you act.

4. **Consignor reads contract.** Give completed contract to Consignor and allow time for her to read it. Then, "Is there anything you do not understand?" If no questions or discussion, sign the form first and then ask them to "OK" it.

NOTE. For first-timers, explain the 90-day feature. Stress that it is their obligation to notify store of disposition of items at expiration date.

---

5. <u>Tag **each** item.</u> The heart of a tag system is **COLOR.** The same color tag is used two times a year. Note Exhibit 12.

Each article received in April is tagged with a blue tag. The advantages of this system are:

A. You know instantly the month the article came in since you will not be keeping any items over 90-days...by contract!

B. You know how long an item has been hanging on the rack!

C. You know who the item belongs to since it has the Customer I. D. Number on it. (See Above)

D. The colors help control markdowns since the tag has the Customer I. D Number on it. (See Exhibit 11.)

E. The colors help control special sales. For example, In May, the blue tag receives a 10% mark-down. In June, the blue tag receives a 20% discount.

EXHIBIT 12. Tag Color Codes

```
                 TAG  COLOR  CODE


        MONTH                    COLOR

        January/July             Red

        February/August          Yellow

        March/September          Lavender

        April/October            Blue

        May/November             Orange

        December/June            Green
```

CAUTION: Check with customer before you markdown beyond the 90 day period (assuming they have not retrieved the article.) Some will permit you to attempt to sell it for 50% off.

Some clients will prefer to donate the items if they have not sold in the 90 day period. In this event, you are free to sell for 50% off, put them on the "Dollar Rack," or whatever.

TIPS

1. **Know your market.** If in Florida, know Florida clothes. Keep sweaters, woolens, etc. for tourists during the tourism months, but do not over-stock. Run such winter items as a special, or treat them as a side-line.

Avoid double-knits and polyesters...they do not sell in Florida. They do not breathe and are quite hot....stay with cotton.

2. **Avoid dated garments.** The item may be in excellent condition, but if it is 20 years old, it isn't going to move. Explain that there are stores which will handle such garments.

3. **When completing the clothing list, be specific!**

COLOR: A light blue suit, not just a blue suit.

SIZE: Be sure the stated size is correct. There is nothing more aggravating for a customer than to try on a size 8 and find out it is a 12. (See Below)

4. **<u>Cautions about bathing suits.</u>** Accept them only if quite new. Only permit "trying on" when wearing undergarments. Make a cute little sign.

5. **<u>Avoid clothing which must be dry cleaned.</u>** Remember the wise shopper. They are in your store because they are trying to stretch their clothing dollar, and they do not want clothing that has added cost to maintain it. If it is a top item, such as silk, they will bend the rule a bit.

6. **<u>Be sure all clothes are on hangers, clean and ironed.</u>** Assume your customers are discriminating. Remember, yours is a boutique.

7. **<u>Shoes cannot be scuffed or dirty.</u>** Insides should be well-kept.

If you permit yourself to accept clothing that does not meet a high standard, it will not move and you will become discouraged. True, a few nice things may look nicer if the majority does not, but this is a false route to follow.

8. **<u>LOST ITEMS.</u>** Items get "lost" when a ticket, unfortunately, comes off. The only solution is to recall who brought the item in. For example, look for another ticketed article of the same color you think was brought in by the same person. Now go to the code

book and trace it.

MORE ABOUT SIZES

Wanda Sieben is an apparel quality researcher at the University of Minnesota. In an article in the BALTIMORE SUN, she says, "In a study of 240 pairs of jeans, the inseam and waist sizes stated on the label often differed significantly from actual measurements."

Fashion is moving away from the long top and full skirt to a more fitted look; thus, size will become a bigger factor in the next few years. The size on the label, however, remains only a starting point. The proof is in the dressing room!

Encourage your customers to "try it on!" Make sure the shoulders fit. If they are correct, the rest of the garment is apt to hang well. Unlike purchasing expensive new fashions, most consignment boutique customers do not wish to fool around with alterations

If a garment is rejected several times, due to "fit," how long do you keep returning it to the rack? This is a judgment call; remember, rack space is precious.

7

ADMINISTRATION

"To business that we love we rise
be-time,
And go to't with delight."
-Shakespeare: Anthony and Cleopatra
V.iv.

KEEPING RECORDS

There are several very good reasons for adopting and maintaining a good system of record-keeping. One, a well-organized system of records, kept up to-date, will save time; It brings order out of disorder.

Two, good records safeguard assets. Accurate cash and inventory records spotlight shortages. Further checking determines the source of the problem.

Three, good records facilitate completion of tax returns and other financial statements which are basic to the operation of a business.

BOOKKEEPING

ASSET: Anything your business owns that has a market value. Cash, purchased apparel and accessories, supplies, furniture, etc.

LIABILITY: Anything your business owes. Notes payable to banks or others, taxes incurred but not paid, wages earned but unpaid, etc.

Assets = Liabilities + Capital

This "accounting equation" is the basis for building your bookkeeping system. Think of CAPITAL as "owner's rights." It is what's left over after subtracting what the creditors have a right to, liabilities from the total business value (assets).

Who will do the bookkeeping? This decision depends largely on two variables. One, do you have the ability? Two, will you have the time?

A computer literate person, equipped with a personal computer and a basic business software package (such as Quicken) can handle the job. If this is not your case, it might be a good idea to retain an accountant to tell you what basic records must be kept, then let him do the work.

TAXES

A wise man once urged, "Have courage and face the facts!" Was he referring to the small business owner? Awesome as it might appear, the following list of taxes may not be complete. It is not uncommon for a city to levy an income tax. A county might enact a sales tax.

Do not despair....if you have neither the time, inclination nor patience to tackle this "paper trail," there are accounting and bookkeeping firms. As mentioned earlier, they offer a menu of services to meet your needs. Farm out what you don't want to do and deduct the cost as a business expense.

EMPLOYER I. D. NUMBER: If you are going to be a sole proprietor with NO employees, your SOCIAL SECURITY number is your employer I. D. number. Otherwise, call Internal Revenue Service and request a "New Business" Kit; it will instruct you how to proceed. (A toll-free IRS number is listed in the "U. S. Government" section of the local phone book.)

FEDERAL INCOME TAX: If a partnership, you must file a Partnership Information Return. Corporations file a separate return and pay their own tax.

EMPLOYEE TAXES AND SOCIAL SECURITY (FICA): Circular E, Publication 15, will tell the employee how to calculate the dollar amount to be withheld. In turn, a completed W-4 Form is filed with you.

The W-9 Form is used by the employee to convey the Social Security number to you. Form 941 is used to remit withheld taxes and FICA, quarterly.

Understand when and how to use the W-2 and 1099 forms.

STATE INCOME TAX: Not all states levy an income tax. If yours does, check the State Department of Revenue for detail and filing instructions. (They are Listed in the "State Government" section of the local phone directory).

SALES TAX: If you are opening your business in a state which has sales or use taxes, prepare to collect and remit them.

First step: contact the State Department of Revenue. Request an application form and remittance instructions. It is not uncommon for some states to require a deposit or a bond.

Note: It may be advisable to take this step <u>after</u> you are operating.

UNEMPLOYMENT COMPENSATION TAX: Applicable only when you have employees. Federal taxes apply when you have paid over $1,500 wages in a quarter or when you have had at least one employee for twenty weeks. Your state also levies a tax.

Even though there may not be employees in the beginning, it is wise to apprise oneself of the <u>current</u> requirements of the law. Prepare for growth.

TANGIBLE AND/OR INTANGIBLE PROPERTY TAX: These are state taxes which may or may not apply in your state. Check it out.

MUNICIPAL LICENSE: Most cities require a retail store license, or occupational license, of some kind. When applying for the license, you should inquire about any other local taxes which may affect your business.

INSURANCE

Your business, like others, will have exposure to risk (probable loss). It is your responsibility to evaluate risk which is too great to bear alone; transfer it to an insurance company for a stipulated premium charge.

CHOOSING AN AGENT: Business growth should bring expanded knowledge of risk management. In the beginning, pick a good agent and let him teach you.

Essentially, there are two kinds of agents. The "Company" agent sells only coverage written by his company. The "Independent" agent represents several companies and their lines of coverage. Both can be competitive.

From whom do you buy Auto and/or Homeowner policies? Is that person knowledgeable about business coverage? If not, check with merchants in the immediate vicinity. Who do they recommend?

Nimi's agent was a tenant in the same strip

center. His lease differed little from hers. This can be an advantage if the landlord insists on certain coverage to protect his assets.

CHOOSING THE COVERAGE: Ask the agent of choice to explain a "Business Owner's Policy." Unless the boutique is located in an extremely hazardous area, such a start-up plan can usually be put together for $250 quarterly premium.

With growth and expansion, investigate another coverage, such as comprehensive general liability, fire and extended coverage, burglary, bailee policy, inland marine, workers's compensation, health insurance, dental insurance, and life insurance.

SECURITY

Simply put, security is the quality, state, or condition of being safe! This applies to your person, your premises, your merchandise and your money.

Unfortunately, no one needs a lecture today on the problems wrought by crime. Presumably, your boutique will not be located in a high-crime neighborhood but, take it for granted, crime is running rampant--you will not be exempt!

Business crime, like fashion, comes in many styles and varieties. The five main crimes are:

- bad checks
- burglary
- embezzlement
- robbery
- shoplifting and/or employee pilferage.

It is suggested you secure the following booklets from the Small Business Administration for study. (See Bibliography for address).

No. 3994   Preventing Retail Theft

No. 3005   Stock Control for Small Stores

No. 3006   Reducing Shoplifting Losses

No. 3007   Preventive Burglary and Loss

No. 3008   Outwitting Bad- Check Passers

No. 3009   Preventing Embezzlement

BAD CHECKS: Defense against bad-check passers rests in procedures you establish and FOLLOW!

1. Take only printed checks (with name,address and phone number) drawn on a local bank.

2. Limit the amount of the check.

3. Obtain positive identification.

BURGLARY: It is unlawful entry. Follow these principles:

- Good lighting inside and out.
- Keyed dead-bolt locks on front and rear doors.
- Good key control.
- An alarm system.
- An adequate money safe.
- Reasonable police patrol.

EMBEZZLEMENT: When you have one or more employees, this area of crime becomes a possibility. Develop a system of money control that can be administered tightly and constantly. Remember, a system with exceptions is no longer a system!

ROBBERY: The taking of property by use of force, violence or fear. Keep only a small amount of cash on hand. Stay calm. Remember, your life is more important than any tangible object in your store!

SHOPLIFTING AND EMPLOYEE PILFERAGE: the best control against shoplifting is YOUR constant awareness and, ultimately, your training of employees to be aware. Nothing can take the place of vigilance. Here are a few tips:

- Watch for loose-fitting coats, shoulder bags, arm slings, totes, unfolded umbrellas, and shopping bags.
- Have a dressing room procedure so you know what goes in AND WHAT COMES OUT!
- Make liberal use of mirrors.
- Beware groups of shoppers.
- Be alert during distractions.

And, don't forget crimes of tag-switching and fake markdowns--both can cost you a bundle. Fasten tickets securely. Use a consistent markdown system, such as the one described in Chapter 8.

The threat of employee pilferage requires YOUR constant vigilance. President Ronald Reagan used a phrase about treaties that also applies here, "Trust--but VERIFY!"

8

SALES PROMOTION

"All progress has resulted from people who took
unpopular positions."
-Adlai Stevenson, speech,
March 22, 1954

ADVERTISING: a paid form of presentation or promotion of goods, services or ideas.

PROMOTION: stimulating demand for goods by advertising, publicity and special events to attract attention and create interest among customers.

In other words, advertising is a form of SALES PROMOTION....and SALES PROMOTION is a never ending process. The key is having a plan and staying organized. Avoid impulsive spending.

A long-range promotional plan should answer several vital questions. What image am I trying to build? What are the best ways to reach my potential customers? How much time and money can I afford to spend on sales promotion?

In the long run, the word-of-mouth referral from a satisfied customer is always the best form of sales promotion. It takes time but will start happening sooner than one thinks. Keeping standards up and performance high stimulates referrals.

SALES, SPECIAL EVENTS, AND STUFF!

Construct a <u>Sales Promotion Calendar</u> and make it your number one planning tool. A sample is shown in Exhibit 15. Add those dates which may be important in your local community. The local Chamber of Commerce or Tourist Bureau should be able to help.

NOTE: Some dates are fixed by statute, others by proclamation. Some vary year to year, such as Easter Sunday. For a more complete listing and specific dates, please consult <u>Clare's Annual Events.</u> It is published by Contemporary Books, 180 North Michi-

---

gan, Chicago, IL 60601. A copy may be in the reference section of your local library.

Targeting sales and promotional effort around such events can be profitable. Another method is to search the local newspaper files and determine how local merchants have built their special sales events.

Transfer selected data to a large wall calendar. Now you have a skeleton SALES PROMOTION plan for the year.

Much of the enjoyment of running your store is wrapped up in sales promotion. In case the imagination runs dry, it is a good idea to subscribe to a NEWSLETTER such as the one published by Kate Holmes in Columbus, OH. Many consignment store owners share sales ideas.

FASHION SHOWS

Conducting fashion shows can become part and parcel of your operation--or, used sporadically as a sales promotion device.

Nimi says, "We used fashion shows as a supplementary income device. We let condo, town house and mobile home park associations and other community groups know that we would love to put on their annual fashion show.

"These can be done evenings, week-ends--we even did some for morning coffee clutches.

"Charging a fee is optional. We never did because we felt we made it up by attracting additional customers. Use the ladies of the club as models. Get them involved. Actually, most models would end up buying the outfit they modeled.

"This filled in many slow weeks. You are not waiting for people to come in the door, you are creating business! Of course, you still keep the doors open."

MARKDOWNS

The colored tag system (see Chapter 6) puts in place a method of handling markdowns. For example, a BLUE tag is put on all items accepted in February. On April 1, a sign is posted atop a rack at the front of the store which says, "All BLUE Tags -- 20% OFF!"

The sign might also list other colors and their discounts. This eliminates the practice of having to re-mark individual garments for each sale.

It also checkmates the dishonest customers--who like to pull their red felt-tip pen and, on the sly, perform their own markdown!

MONTHLY PLAN SESSION

Mark a date on your calendar approximately one week before the end of each month. This is the MONTHLY PLANNING DATE. It is at this time, each month, you will isolate yourself from interruptions and plan the sales promotion of your boutique for the coming month. Select which event, or events, to be used. Also select the promotion tool, or tools, for the job.

Incidentally, many other functions will also be planned during this session. It becomes a ritual. It feels so good to be well-organized!

TIP: Pick up a pad of blank monthly calendar sheets at the local office supply store. They are super for doing the monthly plan.

FLYERS, BULLETINS, ETC.

It is not necessary to own a personal computer (and desk-top publishing software) to prepare effective hand-outs. Exhibit No. 14 shows an APRIL FOOLS DAY announcement from TJ's. Nancy Robinson says it worked!

TIP: Investigate Helen Gregory's book, <u>How to Make Newsletters, Brochures, and Other Good Stuff Without a Computer System.</u> It can be ordered from Pinstripe Publishing, P. O. Box 711, Sedro Woolley, WA 98284.

ADVERTISING

Paid advertising is one of the tools in your SALES PROMOTION tool box. Develop the ad campaign carefully within the framework of your SALES PROMOTION CALENDAR and budget.

NEWSPAPER

Do you have a community newspaper? Initially, skip the large, expensive, metropolitan daily.

Display ad vs classified? The advertising budget often makes the decision. Study both types in the paper you select. Where are other consignment stores advertising? Time spent investigating can often pay great dividends.

Can you write a good ad? If concerned, where can you get help? A poorly worded ad is a waste of money. Study other ads. What message are they trying to deliver to potential customers?

Several small ads usually pull more customers than a large, more expensive ad. Nimi says, "I had a $25.00 ad which ran in the local BEACON--week after week after week. That averaged over $100 per month and that is a lot of money. But, it was worth it. It brought me business."

YELLOW PAGES

Kate Holmes, who started her store "One More Time" in Columbus, Oh, in 1975, says, "Yellow Pages advertising definitely helps your business. The problem is, under what category will your potential customer look?"

Look through your own Yellow pages. Who lists

where? In Pinellas County, Florida (we have a county-wide yellow page book), the following number of stores were listed under the available categories.

Clothing (Bought and Sold)	5
Clothing (Used)	1
Consignment Service	60
Second Hand Stores	8
Thrift Shops	35

"Consignment Services" is where the action is in the Clearwater-St. Pete area. The "Thrift Shops" category was composed primarily of charitable and religious stores. To add perspective, Pinellas County's population is 851,659. The Tampa Bay metro area exceeds two million people.

Boxed ads were infrequent; could it be the cost? Should you enter the Yellow Pages from start-up? For the most simple listing you are looking at $25 per month. Will your budget allow it? Or, does good judgment dictate postponement?

TIP: Check with your Yellow Pages to see if they still offer a free one-liner.

EXHIBIT 13. Newspaper Tie-in Ad

EXHIBIT 14. April Fool's Day Flyer

WELCOME TO T.J.'s APRIL FOOLS DAY SALE!

Lavender & White Tags	10% OFF
Yellow Tags	20% OFF
Pink Tags	50% OFF
Green Tags	60% OFF

All Shoes and Belts - 10% OFF

Items on "SALE" Rack are as marked on tags, regardless of color.

Happy Seeking & Finding !

T.J.'s UNIQUE BOUTIQUE
9148 Seminole Blvd.
397-1073

EXHIBIT 15. Sales Promotion Calendar

SALES PROMOTION CALENDAR

JANUARY
New Year's Day; Martin Luther King, Jr. Day; Three Kings Day (Puerto Rico); Battle of New Orleans (Louisiana); Robert E. Lee Day.

FEBRUARY
Lincoln's Birthday; Washington's Birthday; President's Day; Valentine's Day; Georgia Day; Ground Hog Day; National Freedom Day; Susan B. Anthony Day.

MARCH
St. Patrick's Day; Palm Sunday; Passover; Easter; Texas Independence Day; Mardi Gras Day; Thomas Jefferson's Birthday (Alabama); San Jacinto Day (Texas).

APRIL
April Fool's Day; (Check religious holidays in April each year); Arbor Day; Bird Day; Pan American Day; Verrazano Day.

MAY
Mother's Day; Armed Forces Day; Memorial Day; Loyalty Day; May Day; National Maritime Day; Harry S. Truman's Birthday (Missoui).

JUNE
Flag Day; Father's Day; Jefferson Davis Birthday; King Kamehamecha Day (Hawaii); Emancipation Day (Texas); West Virginia D

JULY
Fourth of July; Colorado Day; Bennington Battle Day (Vermont); Pioneer Day (Utah); Puerto Rico Constitution Day; Huey P. Long Day (Louisiana)

AUGUST

SEPTEMBER
Labor Day, Rosh Hashannah; Citizenship Day; Grandparent's Day; Defender's Day ((Maryland).

OCTOBER
Columbus Day; United Nations Day; Halloween; Child's Health Day; General Pulaski Memorial Day; Reformation Day; World Poetry Day; Alaska Day.

NOVEMBER
Election Day; Veteran's Day; Thanksgiving Day; Elizabeth Clay Stanton Day; Sadie Hawkins Day; Wright Brothers Day; All Saints Day.

DECEMBER
Hanukkah; Christmas Day; New Year's Eve; Bill of Rights Day; Forefather's Day.

9

EMPLOYEES

"Tact is the ability to describe others
as they see themselves."

-Abraham Lincoln

President Lincoln was not speaking specifically about employees, but it fits; dealing with people is an art form.

Recruitment and retention of good employees is a requirement of a growing business. Just when you will feel the need for your first employee rests in your judgment alone.

When the time arrives, here are important steps to take.

JOB DESCRIPTION

What do you want this person to do? Be specific.. Sell, tag articles, straighten racks, open the shop, or sweep the floors? How many hours will she work? What days? What will you pay? When?

Putting a job description on paper will assure two things; one, you will know what you want her to do and, as importantly, SHE WILL KNOW! In other words, you'll both be on the same page. It should be a profitable relationship for each.

PREPARE BOOKKEEPING

If you have an accountant, ask what has to be done. If not, now is a good time to consider engaging one to help you.

Otherwise, do some homework. This first experience handling payroll, taxes and Social Security should not frighten you. It is part of business growth and is to be expected sooner or later.

CAUTION! Do not rush out and hire an employee before doing your homework.

SALARY

You should be able to hire the right lady for minimum wage. If you are not sure of the current hourly rate, ask a fellow merchant or call the Wage and Hour Division of the U. S. Department of Labor.

BENEFITS

It is not customary to offer fringe benefits to part-time employees. Even if your first employee is full-time, there is no need to rush into benefit programs.

As the store grows, make a study of fringe benefit programs and incorporate your determination into the Annual Business Plan (See Chapter f10).

TRAINING

Are you going to hire an experienced person? Finding someone with retail sales experience should not be too difficult. The advantage is obvious if the experience was good experience. Otherwise, you are hiring all the bad habits accumulated during poor experience.

Hiring the inexperienced person means you must be responsible for some initial training. Go back to the written "Job Description." What the person does will dictate the training to be provided.

Preparing to train a new employee, full- or part-time, can be beneficial. There is an old axiom: the teacher often profits more than the student!

In every instance, be prepared to give rudimentary instruction in such basics as handling the cash register, learning the racks, re-stocking garments, etc.

10

THE BUSINESS PLAN

"He who sails without a chart
may well return without a ship!"

-Anonymous

THE BUSINESS PLAN is a document prepared by you for YOU! It is a road map to follow in the conduct of your business. It is up-dated annually.

The plan, which contains your personal resume, business goals, budget, market analysis and action steps, is always called for by a banker when you approach for a loan. Most banks will not consider a loan application without an accompanying business plan.,

The plan will help you become a better manager of the boutique. The mere fact you have taken the time to put a coherent plan on paper evidences the first step to good management. You have a track to run on. An old adage, "If the idea is not on paper, it is nothing more than a dream."

PREPARING THE PLAN

1. <u>Write **or** rewrite **your** personal resume.</u> If, per chance, you have never done one, there are a number of books in your local library which will assist in organizing personal history.

2. <u>Re-read **the** preceding **chapters and** start making--and recording--vital decisions.</u> Organize these into sections titled:

Business Goals,

Budget,

Market Analysis,

Action Steps.

When completed, you have a business plan.

Can you get by without preparing a business plan? Of course--for awhile. But, why run the risk of a trial-and-error overload? Why not carefully chart the course for your journey?

START-UP COST PLUS

This subject is purposely placed at the rear of the book. Each item contained in the Start-up Cost for YOUR Boutique is treated in the preceding chapters.

The amounts will, quite naturally, vary with each start-up. You should, however, be able to attach your figures to the checklist on page 91.

CAPITALIZATION

In addition to start-up capital, there are other reasons to have a reserve fund. Call it all your "initial capitalization." Look upon it as money to be used, if necessary, the first year. If these dollars are not set aside, earmarked for the business, you can be putting yourself under tremendous pressure.

How much capital? One simple method of calculation: one year rent! In the hypothetical case above, $10,000 would do it. Another method: 2 times start-up cost, or around $7,500. Opening the doors with only enough for start-up cost could make for a perilous trip!

What if a medical emergency strikes and help is needed to run the shop? Note: No allocation was made in the above example for employees. It is assumed you and your family members can handle it initially. What if the boutique gets off to a slow start? How long can you hang in there without closing the doors?

Where does the capital come from? Generally, it is from personal savings. If not available, it must be borrowed from somewhere.

When raising money, think in terms of either "debt financing" or "equity financing."

Debt financing is a loan. Family, friends, commercial bank, credit union, savings and loan (Home Equity Loan) or other loan companies. The lender evaluates your chances of succeeding in the business, charges an appropriate interest rate on the loan, and expects the note to be paid when due.

Equity financing means you give up some ownership in the business. The other party gambles on your ability to make a profit and expects a share of it as a return on the investment. Giving away part ownership is usually considered a last resort, but

EXHIBIT 16: Start-up Cost

```
                    START-UP COST


                                          YOUR
CHAP    ITEM                    COST?     COST?


 2      Rent*                   1,600     _____
 2      Attorney Fees              30     _____
 3      Sign                      500     _____
 3      Dressing Rooms            300     _____
 3      Clothing Racks            400     _____
 3      Shelving                  300     _____
 3      Hangers                    50     _____
 3      Office Supplies            30     _____
 3      Printing                  200     _____
 3      Misc. Supplies            100     _____
 3      Credit Card Equip.        100     _____
 4      Purchased Inventory       400     _____
 7      Insurance                 200     _____
 8      Advertising               100     _____
 3      Sales Counter              50     _____
        _____  _____
        _____  _____
        _____  _____
        _____  _____

        TOTAL                 $3,800     _____

*First Month + Deposit
```

sometimes it can be the perfect solution. This might be the case when the new owner has a particular skill which is useful to the business and agrees to work in the business.

NOTES

EXHIBIT 17. Nancy Robinson works with a customer--
What it is all about!

11

THE CUSTOMER IS QUEEN

CUSTOMER ORIENTED: describing the effort to comprehend the reasons, desires, and problems of the customer with the intent to use this information in fulfilling the customer's needs, and hopefully to increase sales and profits.
-From the <u>Dictionary</u> of <u>Business</u>
<u>and</u> <u>Management.</u>

Would "Queen for a Day" be a better title for this chapter? Whatever the label, the definition of customer orientation is the main focus.

Ken Meyer comments, "In my years of recruiting and training insurance sales people, I found their major motivator to be a sincere desire to help the customer. It bordered on catering. The good ones really enjoyed helping others."

Contrast this to the negative image of today's

retail sales person. Too often, they display an attitude of "I just don't want to be bothered." Fortunately, good service still abounds in the small specialty shops. It is the one advantage they have over the large discount houses.

One thing is certain; in YOUR CONSIGNMENT BOUTIQUE, you will have 100% control to create the image the customer perceives! At least, until employees are hired.

RETURNS OR REFUNDS

No! For the simple reason, you have paid the Consignor for the article. When allowing a return, you lose your profit by paying twice.

Nimi says, "There is one exception. We occasionally had people shop for others-- like in a nursing home, etc. In such a case, we gave them until day's end to return the articles. We wanted to be fair.

"We also had an exchange policy. Since we had already paid the Consignor, we allowed the customer to exchange the article for another of equal amount."

LAYAWAY

Nimi says, "We permitted layaway's. We required 20% down and pick-up within 30 days. The latter was necessary since we had to pay the Consignor within the contract terms.

"It was a great service, especially for the working woman. I found the single parent also purchased more items this way."

There are also disadvantages. Space requirements. Forfeited sales--if not taken, is it fair to the consignor? Who gets the forfeited money? Think it through carefully.

CREDIT CARDS

From a customer relations point of view, having Visa/Mastercard is a must.

Nimi says, "I found our greatest use of credit sales was to the tourists. They just did not carry cash.

"For the tourist, there was the added safety that their purchase was insured should it be lost or stolen enroute home."

STORE HOURS

One, post the store hours prominently and, two, STICK TO THEM!

The hours should fit the market. A store serving a viable working woman's market will need to stay open after 5 PM and, possibly, some on Saturday. The key is to know your major markets and act accordingly. Make it convenient for ladies to stop and shop.

FASHION ADVICE

Nimi Wanek found that one of the most satisfying parts of running a boutique was helping the "regular" dress well. She says, "I find there are certain customers who appreciate your advice and counsel. Once you get to know them, what they do, the events they need to dress for, it is amazing what you can really do for them.

"Another advantage of helping ladies dress well is--once other people tell them how nice they look, you can dress them for the rest of their lives!

"For example, many of my clients were working women. You have to blend personality with the work-

_____

place when recommending the right garb. It is fun.

"No longer must the businesswoman wear the navy blue or gray suit. Nor should our lady lawyer show up in court draped in a large print. Learning what is "in" and what is not is important."

What Nimi touches upon above is loosely called "wardrobe engineering" and a number of "experts" have written on the subject. Perhaps the most noted is John T. Molloy. His book, "The Women's Dress for Success Book." was published in 1977, but is still considered by many to be the thing. It should be in your local library.

Here is a sampling of his observations:

"Women who wear glasses are considered smarter than women who do not.

Brunette women command more authority than blond women.

Gray hair on a man adds authority but gray hair on a woman detracts from her authority.

Ph.D's in general are expected to be atypical dressers." Heard enough to want to check out the book? Or start a CONSIGNMENT BOUTIQUE?

PRIDE OF OWNERSHIP

There are super-sophisticates who might want to label PRIDE OF OWNERSHIP as cornball, yet a sage counters with the fact no one has been able to repeal the laws of human nature.

It is natural to have a surge of emotion, that wonderful feeling of elation and pride, when you open the doors of YOUR OWN business. From the moment you seized the notion it might be possible to the welcome given to the first customer, it has been an adventure.

Now comes the continuing saga---the thrill of amassing experience. How rewarding it will be to own a profitable CONSIGNMENT BOUTIQUE.

GOOD LUCK!

BIBLIOGRAPHY

Albert, Kenneth J., How To Pick the Right Small Busines Opportunity, (McGraw-Hill:NY) 1977.

Black, H. M., Black's Law Dictionary, (West:St. Paul, MN) 1988.

Eaton, P., "Saving Graces," New York, (May 1, 1989) p. 120.

Freese, N. and S. Duncan, How to Start A Consignment Shop & Make it Go, (Sylvan Books:Syracuse, IN) 1984.

Freidman, Marilyn, Consider Consignments: How to Own, Open, and Operate Your Town's Permanent Garage Sale, (Vantage Press) 1979.

Holmes,Kate, To Good To Be Threw: The Complete Operations Manual for Consignment Stores, (Chatham Communications, Inc.) 1988.

Hoopes, Roy, "Mind Your Own Business," Modern Maturity, (Feb-Mar, 1991) p. 26.

Jones, Jan, A Woman's Business: Consignment, (Shellie Press) 1982.

Molloy, John T., The Women's Dress for Success Book, (Follett:Chicago) 1977.

Phillips, Starr, <u>Treasure Transfers: A Resale and Consignment Guide for Orange County, Los Angeles County, and San Diego County</u>, (DC Publishing Co.) 1985.

Robin, R. R., "The Thrift Shop Connection (Contracts with Charities)," <u>Changing Times</u>, (March, 1989) p. 43.

Rosenberg, Jerry M., <u>Dictionary of Business and Management</u>, (John Wiley:NY) 1983.

SCORE, Chapter 115, <u>Small Business Handbook</u>, (Largo, FL) 1986.

Warda, Mark, <u>How to Start a Business in Florida</u>, (Sphinx Publishing:Clearwater, FL) 1983.

Whitis, R. F., <u>Starting and Operating a Vintage Clothing Shop</u>, (Pilot Books:Babylon, NY) 1983.

OTHER INFORMATION SOURCES

Small Business Administration, <u>SBA</u> <u>115A</u> <u>Free</u>
<u>Management</u> <u>Assistance</u> <u>Publications.</u> P. O. Box
15434, Ft. Worth,   TX 76119

<u>Tax</u> <u>Guide</u> <u>For</u> <u>Small</u> <u>Business</u>, Published Annually By
the U.S. Internal Revenue Service

<u>Used/Consigned</u> <u>Clothing</u> <u>Business</u> <u>Guide.</u> Entrepre-
neur, Inc., 2392 Morse Avenue, P. O. Box 19787, Irvine,
CA 92713-9437 ($69.50) Contains step-by-step instruc-
tions for starting a consignment used clothing business.

<u>National</u> <u>Association</u> <u>of</u> <u>Resale</u> <u>and</u> <u>Thrift</u> <u>Shops.</u> c/o
Trudy Miller, 153 Halsted , Chicago Heights, IL 60411.
Founded 1984. 300 Members. Helps members to
establish credit and deal more effectively with bankers;
identify and locate new markets. Annual Convention.
Also sponsors workshops.

INDEX

"CONSIGNMENT BOUTIQUE"

CONSULTING WITH

A

FLAIR !

**For
Detail
Contact:**

NIMI WANEK

**8857 Park Blvd.
St. Petersburg, FL 33708**

(813) 391 1293

TO ORDER ADDITIONAL COPIES

1. Contact your local bookstore. If not in stock, give them the title and ISBN number (located on UPC code--back cover)

<u>or</u>

2. Complete order form below and mail with remittance to **MEYER-MAN BOOKS.**

Please send me _____ copy (ies) of **CONSIGNMENT BOUTIQUE PRIMER** @ $19.95 each (plus $3.00 shipping first book; $2.00 each additional book.) Florida residents please add 7% sales tax. Enclosed is my check or money order. (All foreign orders: write for current price.) Please print:

Name: _____

Street: _____

City: _____ State: ___ Zip: _____

MEYER-MAN BOOKS

10895 Del Prado Drive, E.
Largo, FL 34644-4641